Native Americans

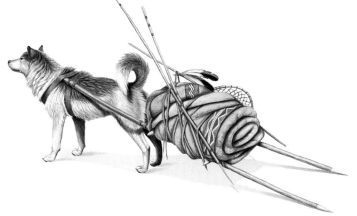

Text: Robert Coupe

Consultant: Colin Sale, Geography Lecturer and Author

This edition first published 2003 by

MASON CREST PUBLISHERS INC.

370 Reed Road

Broomall, PA 19008

© Weldon Owen Inc.

Conceived and produced by

Weldon Owen Pty Limited

Library of Congress Cataloging-in-Publication Data on file at the Library of Congress

ISBN: 1-59084-167-0

Printed in Singapore.

1 2 3 4 5 6 7 8 9 06 05 04 03

CONTENTS

Early Americans   4

How They Moved   6

On the Plains   12

Inside the Tepee   14

Dressing Up   16

Ceremonies   18

Finding Food   22

New Arrivals   28

Glossary   30

Index   31

EARLY AMERICANS

Over 10,000 years ago, the Earth's surface was very different. The seas were much lower, and so there was much more land. The first Americans walked across a frozen land bridge between Asia and North America. They were hunters who searched for herds of animals from Siberia to Alaska.

MOVING SOUTH

From Alaska, the early Native Americans gradually moved south and settled in all parts of North America. Different tribes settled in different places.

Arctic

Northwest Coast

Great Basin

Subarctic

Great Plains

Plateau

Northeast

California

Southwest

Southeast

HOW THEY MOVED

Early Americans used boats for fishing, for going on hunting expeditions, and for carrying things from place to place. Most of their boats were simple and made for traveling only on calm rivers and lakes. Some larger boats, though, like the one on the left with its high prow, could ride larger waves.

DID YOU KNOW?

The Inuit people in the cold Arctic region invented the kayak to use for hunting. Traditional kayaks hold only one person.

DID YOU KNOW?

Native Americans wore snowshoes shaped like bears' paws. These kept them from sinking into the soft snow.

In icy northern areas, people trained native dogs, called huskies, to help them move goods. The dogs' thick fur protected them from the cold. Women carried goods in baskets and children on their back. Men carried spears and other weapons for catching food and fighting any enemies they met on the way.

Working Alone

A single husky can drag a big load on a pair of poles, called a travois.

Teamwork

Teams of huskies can drag very heavy loads on sleds that people make from wood or deer antlers.

9

Spanish explorers brought horses and ponies to the Great Plains of North America more than 400 years ago. Native Americans soon learned to tame and breed horses, and ride them. They used them for hunting, for moving goods, and for riding into battle against other tribes.

War Paint
Before a battle, warriors often painted their horses with bright colors and decorated them with feathers.

Plains pony

Appaloosa horse

On the Move

With the coming of horses, large groups of people could move quickly across the country.

ON THE PLAINS

The people of the Great Plains lived in strong
tentlike buildings called tepees. Tepee camps
were built in a circle, leaving a space on the
east side. If the entrance to a tepee was open,
a visitor was welcome to enter.

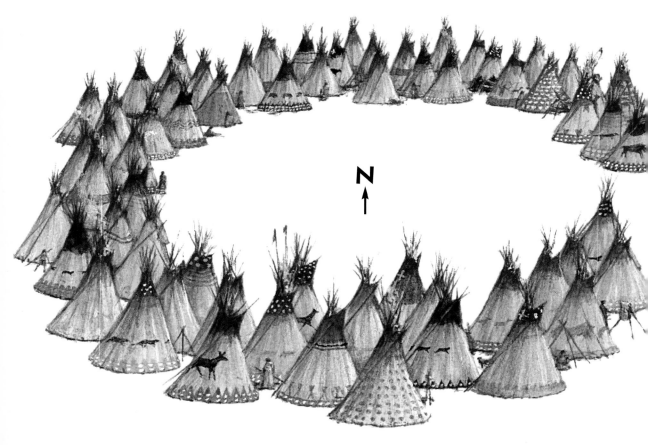

Tepee camp

Shooting Lessons

In most of the Plains-area tribes, young boys learned to hunt with bows and arrows by shooting at still targets.

Pipe Smoking

Like many other groups of Native Americans, Sioux people smoked long pipes in some of their ceremonies.

INSIDE THE TEPEE

Tepees were made of buffalo hide and were held up by strong wooden poles. When a tribe needed to move, the tepees were easily taken down and put up again.

Smoke Flaps
These could be opened from inside.

Inside
There were no separate rooms. Items the family owned were hung from the walls.

Cooking Methods
One way of heating food was to use hot stones.

Entrance
This was covered with a piece of animal skin.

Painted Symbols
These were believed to protect the people who lived inside.

DRESSING UP

Native Americans made their clothes from the skins and furs of animals and from cotton and other plants. They changed what they wore through the year to suit the different seasons. For special occasions they often dressed in colorful, highly decorated clothing.

DID YOU KNOW?

Some Native American men wore headdresses made from eagles' feathers for special ceremonies. This is a Sioux headdress.

Dressed for the Cold
Animal skins, with the fur inside, helped keep out the cold of winter.

Navajo Sand Painting
The Navajo people destroyed the sand painting after a healing ceremony.

CEREMONIES

Native American healers held ceremonies to cure sick people. The Navajo people of the Southwest crushed different-colored rocks to make large sand pictures on the ground during curing ceremonies. They believed these would soak up or reverse a person's illness.

SAND PAINTING IN A JAR

1 Add different colors of food coloring to piles of sand.

2 Pour layers of different-colored sand into a jar until it is full.

3 Make designs by pushing a thin stick up and down the inside edge of the jar. Screw the lid on tight to keep your painting safe.

People believed that dancing helped them hunt, grow crops, and recover from illnesses. The Hopi people, from the southwestern desert, brought live snakes to the priests for one type of ceremony. The priests performed a complicated and dangerous snake dance to make it rain and help the crops to grow.

DID YOU KNOW?

Hopi people performed a buffalo dance to bring good luck for a hunt. The dancer wore a buffalo horn on his head.

FINDING FOOD

Hunters on horseback chased herds of buffalo on the Great Plains. Some men used long spears, others shot with bows and arrows. Native Americans used almost every part of the animals they killed. They even made toys for their children out of the bones and hoofs. The hides provided clothing for cold weather and the flesh gave them meat.

LAND AND SEA

A few Inuit people still use bows and arrows to hunt polar bears and deer on land, and harpoons to kill seals and walruses in the sea.

Food from the Land

People grew crops such as corn and chili peppers, and ate other vegetables, nuts, and wild fruit.

Finding food was easier in areas where there was water. People often hid among reeds and caught or shot ducks and other water birds. Sometimes they trapped birds in nets. They also hunted rabbits, deer, and even insects. In some places people settled for long periods and became farmers.

Drying Out
People dried fruit and vegetables, such as gourds, so they would have enough for the winter months when food was hard to find.

Native Americans who lived close to the coast hunted seals, whales, and large ocean fish from boats. They also collected oysters and other shellfish. In inland streams, people trapped salmon in large handheld nets.

NETS AND SPEARS

Native Americans used spears to catch salmon and other fish. On the Great Lakes in the Northeast, hunters set nets to catch fish during the day and speared them at night.

Reservations
Many Native Americans were forced to live in areas set aside for them, called reservations.

NEW ARRIVALS

More than 200 years ago, settlers from Europe began to spread out across North America. They fought battles with Native American tribes. The newcomers forced the Native Americans to leave the lands on which they had lived for centuries.

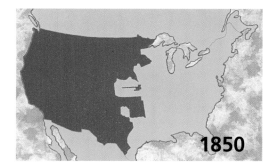

1850

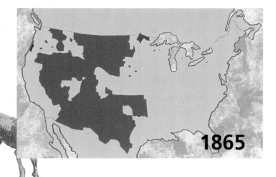

1865

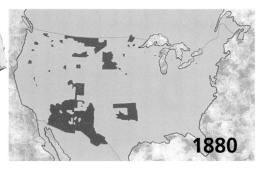

1880

Maps of Land Lost
The dark parts show
Native American land.
You can see how much
they have lost over
the past 150 years.

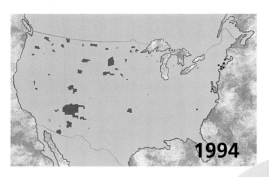

1994

GLOSSARY

Arctic The part of the Earth near the North Pole. The most northern parts of North America, Europe, and Asia are part of the Arctic.

gourd A kind of fruit that has a hard skin. When the skin of a gourd is dried, it can be used as a bowl or a bottle.

harpoon A sharp, spearlike weapon that is attached to the end of a rope.

Inuit The name of some of the people who live in the Arctic. Inuit is a Native American word that means "people."

kayak A canoe that is covered to keep waves from washing in. Traditional kayaks are built to hold one person. Inuit people invented the kayak.

INDEX

boats   6–7, 26

buffalo   21, 23

clothing   16–17, 23

cooking   15

dancing   20–21

farming   24–25

fishing   7, 26–27

headdresses   17

healing   18–19, 20

horses   10–11, 23

hunters and hunting   4, 7, 8, 10,
13, 20–21, 22–23, 25, 26

huskies   8–9

kayaks   7

reservations   28

sand painting   18–19

snowshoes   8

tepees   12, 14–15

PICTURE AND ILLUSTRATION CREDITS

BOOKS IN THIS SERIES

WEIRD AND WONDERFUL WILDLIFE

Incredible Creatures
Creepy Creatures
Scaly Things
Feathers and Flight
Attack and Defense
Snakes
Hidden World
Reptiles and Amphibians
Mini Mammals
Up and Away
Mighty Mammals
Dangerous Animals

LAND, SEA, AND SKY

Sharks and Rays
Underwater Animals
Mammals of the Sea
Ocean Life
Volcanoes
Weather Watching
Maps and Our World
Earthquakes
The Plant Kingdom
Rain or Shine
Sky Watch
The Planets

INFORMATION STATION

Every Body Tells a Story
The Human Body
Bright Ideas
Out and About
Exploring Space
High Flying
How Things Work
Native Americans
Travelers and Traders
Sports for All
People from the Past
Play Ball!